UP IN NATHANAEL'S ROOM

Eileen Erikson

This book is provided courtesy of the **Amelia Island Book Festival's Authors in Schools Literacy Program,** made possible through the generosity of these donors and sponsors.

Presenting & Platinum: Wm. L. Amos, Sr. Foundation ~ Anonymous Donor *in Loving Memory of Shiela Fountain* ~ CBC National Bank ~ WISH YOU WELL FOUNDATION ~ Rick & Hollie Keffer
Gold: David Miller Family ~ Artistic Florist
Silver: Bk of America-Merrill Lynch-Wealth Management—*Park, Houston, North Group* ~ Debonair ~ Kinder Morgan-Nassau Terminals ~ Elsa Mitschele & Michael Waskew *in Loving Memory of Erika Brodsky* ~ OnlineBinding.Com ~ Ottima Group: *Mark & Marie Fenn* ~ Rayonier Advanced Materials ~ Anne & Larry Read ~ Walmart ~ WestRock
Bronze: Green Biz~Institute for Enterprise, Inc.~Focus Investment Banking: *Fran & George Shea*~ Barb & Bruce Heggenstaller~The Book Loft ~FL Writers Assn Fndn~Ken&Vickie Lanier~Betsy & Rod Odom
Other: Aim South ~ Kiwanis Club ~ Newcomers Book Club-Book Bags ~ GCAI Book Club ~ Oceanside Cleaners ~ the UPS Store ~ Amelia Audiology ~ Amelia Dental Group ~ Art on Centre ~ John & Brenda Carr ~ King's Plumbing & Home Repair ~ Parker Contracting Inc. ~ Bobby Ramsay ~ T-Ray's ~ Steve Johnson Automotive ~ Jim & Peggy Weinsier
For a complete list of donors and members please visit our website
www.ameliaislandbookfestival.org

AuthorHouse™
1663 Liberty Drive
Bloomington, IN 47403
www.authorhouse.com
Phone: 1-800-839-8640

First published by AuthorHouse 8/31/2009

ISBN: 978-1-4490-0385-2 (sc)

Printed in the United States of America
Bloomington, Indiana

This book is printed on acid-free paper.

authorHOUSE®

FORWARD AND DEDICATION

When our grandson Nathanael was born, February 12, 2004, we were so excited, we rushed to Ohio from Florida, bearing gifts, many gifts. Of course all of his parents friends and other family members did the same. Everyone rushed to see him when he got home from the hospital and, of course, to see his room. My daughter, his mother, kept saying "no more, please," but it seemed to fall on deaf ears. Thus, his grandmother thought up this story. I hope you enjoy reading this book to your children and grandchildren and please note my grandson's interpretation of the things in his room. At only 4 years old, he adds to the illustrations in his very own book and invites the readers and audience to draw the things in their rooms. This book is dedicated to my sweet grandson, now known as Nate.

Up in Nathanael's room, is a beautiful bed and a crib and a sled.

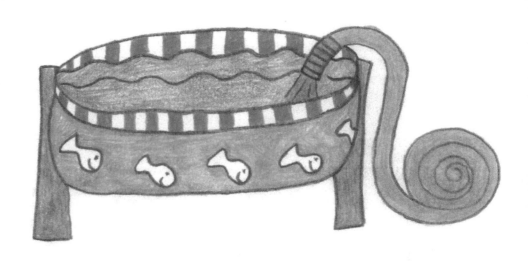

Up in Nathanael's room are blankets and clothes

and a tub with a hose

Up in Nathanael's room, are hats and bears and
bats and chairs.

Up in Nathanael's room, are caps and maps and balls and cats.

Up in Nathanael's room, is dad and mom and

Ruby and Tom.

WA WAAAA!

Up in Nathanael's room are books and toys and

sometimes noise.

Up in Nathanael's room is a cross from Aunt Shelley and petroleum jelly.

Up in Nathanael's room is grandmother and

grand-dad and a changing pad.

Up in Nathanael's room is a rocking chair, but
the boy's not there.

He can't get into his room.

Nate draws some objects in his room

Nathaneel

Nate
RAT

BALL
Nathanae

Nate invites you to draw the things

in your room.